LETTERS

IN A

BRUISED

COSMOS

*

ALSO BY LIZ HOWARD

Infinite Citizen of the Shaking Tent

LETTERS IN A BRUISED COSMOS

LIZ HOWARD

McCLELLAND & STEWART

McClelland & Stewart and colophon are registered trademarks of Penguin Random House Canada Limited.

Published simultaneously in the United States of America.

Library and Archives Canada Cataloguing in Publication data is available upon request.

ISBN: 978-0-7710-3757-3
ebook ISBN: 978-0-7710-3758-0

Book design by Leah Springate
Cover image based on "NGC 6357" composite (X-ray: NASA/CXC/PSU/L.Townsley et al; Optical: UKIRT; Infrared: NASA/JPL-Caltech), pixelsorted by Zach Whalen. See more at twitter.com/crookedcosmos

Typeset in Centaur by M&S, Toronto
Printed in Canada

McClelland & Stewart,
a division of Penguin Random House Canada Limited,
a Penguin Random House Company
www.penguinrandomhouse.ca

3 4 5   25 24 23 22

Penguin
Random House
McCLELLAND & STEWART

CONTENTS

A new being comes into the world for a second time, out of a deep cut that opens in a biography.

— CATHERINE MALABOU, *Ontology of the Accident,*
An Essay on Destructive Plasticity

LETTERS

IN A

BRUISED

COSMOS

*

PROBABILITY CLOUD

The universe broadcasts its lifespan in radiant heat. I need to believe my

account will outpace its ending. Technical oracle, a feed that repeats itself,

a reckoning. What I felt was complete disorientation. But the ~~night~~ sky is

more than a map to read into the end and origin of everything. There is

a guilt that folds into me like   **THE**   humanity. A darkness in the

                                           HOLE

signal. A mark science confides   **IN THE**   is evidence of another universe,

the collision of an afterbirth.   **SKY**   If I continue can I hold the

body beyond its contact traces of violation and intimacy? The palimpsest

furniture of our specious present, a succession of excess. I am here after all

for decadence and silence. See this decadence—a bloom beneath the skin

of my invitation.

                Not truth but surface.

SUPERPOSITION

I've gone too far
and now I'm over
my head in the river.
Its rapids stained
red with tannins
leached from the decay
of wood and other plant
matter, lilies and reeds.
Kebsquasheshing
'river of weeds'
bifurcating its way
north to the Arctic.
I'm six and unable
to swim, my small
limbs pushing against
the crosscurrent
feet waterlogged
in the silt.
The overcast
sun seems
to make the water
hum its colour,
something cousin
to blood.
In the developing
mind to think
a thing is to
make it happen.
This is the end

then here below
        the surface. A voice
            shooting through me
            like a warning,
                a dark closing in
                    with the storm clouds
                when another
            swimmer grabs hold
        of me and drags
    me back up

to the light.

SETTLER——ANISHINAABEKWE——NOLI TURBARE

Beauty is my irreparable eye

and today I became geometric.

A faux linear figure that distills

a skip trace of first principles.

In a whiteout of Atlantic snow,

banging stars into the femoral vein

of Euclid while rows of lavender

circuits, all porous, surrounded me.

I genuflected before the hospital

parking lot of my father's jaundice,

for I am a good daughter

of the colony.

The colony which begot

the immortal heart of the markets.

Resources nursed all young bucks

of the florets, a liquidity I should service

or else receive a lesser dessert.

With my smudge cleanse at the ready

I find myself dispensing with the usual

future haunt of resilience. A survival

signalling my relationship to time,

or am I out of it entirely?

Come polygon and I circumvent

the disaster, *do not disturb my circles.*

Holy I went, holy all around my head,

the holy I am went careening

down the back stairs of this low-rise

rental. Striated by the pinnacle light

of this city that has my blood pooled

purple at the center of its gravity.

You can scan the ground from overhead

for death pits. I read this on the internet

when I was dehydrated, lonely, and afraid.

Office plants became the broad-leafed

repositories for my cognition's fated heart.

I've gone and been abominable.

A column extended from the top

of my head into heaven.

At the edges of my system

an Anishinabek or Indo-European

projection of words my nerves

could translate into the crawlspace

of animal magnetism.

White pine verticals send us up

as a stomach pumped by filial love.

Oh, inconsequent curb of my street

I refuse to kneel. This day like any other.

Plush pockets of rust about another

falsehood of water, a creek that pleats.

I've gone and got a blister. That summer

a black bear's muzzle got coated

in shellac from the aerosol can she bit

through on my mother's porch at the edge

of the forest. Four generations ago,

my great-grandmother said, don't ever

shoot a black bear, they are my people.

Makwa, makwa from the north shore.

Before I continue to speak more than this

mortuary sunrise where I am only just alive.

Boozhoo.

Aaniin.

Hello.

Today is over.

I DREAM IN GMAIL

PMS winter solstice, the hereditary gist of a fractal
interior. I buried another yesterday by the back door
of this expanding universe just before I dreamt in Gmail.
As if all new visions visit digitally: a reply all *cri de coeur*
from Athens, a bcc-promoted punk tour streamed via a cave
system linked to the romantic history of strange quarks.
Spooky action at a distance. I slid down a snow bank into a
northern stream and then you smiled as if you like me now,
now that my ass is wet. At midnight that stream became the
border between New France and my dream of being intelligible.
Then I'm awake in the garage with my firstborn thought.
A thought that sublimates into a braid of snowflakes.
What could offer me an office in the February pension:
a warmth that only makes its way into the deepest
pockets. A novice love that can't help but become
a flight risk.

STANZA AS INFINITY FILTER

A room with a view

summer holidays digressing

into the heartstrings of a bad faith

chorus. Along the balcony of our latter

days each subatomic thrum is a past

note there's no coming back from.

The full self of forest mushrooms

before rot sets in. The reward centre

of minor sins, post-present. A tender

pressure against the caul or thin

gauze of skin infinity filters through

and finds us human. Nothing but rain

for days, my id a sump pump, so I'll not

argue with the weather. I'm already lost

to the hard plumb of a liquid centre

a dead ringer for the first-person singular

on my knees and partially dressed

as you'd have it. But I'm outside of this

waiting for my arraignment

within expression while the lights

along my street are leaking beams

teething a sodium brace along the base

of my skull. Grave-to-cradle cap over

a brainstem I can't slap for blooming

a draft I'd never have picked.

My wet cells kindling another

mirror, the sense-presence of you.

As in childhood false promises flew

with the summer wind through poplars

snapping every leaf of those august trees.

The stars aren't keeping track but I know

how to score this. I don't forgive you

and you don't need to be forgiven.

My mistrusted *I* velvet fastened

to whatever happens. Such is the feeling

as the moon rises perpendicular to my view

outside of time and half-bred consequence

you can't send me back to my room.

AS IF OUR FUTURE PAST BORE A BAD ALGORITHM

A few particles ambushed the past
I opened my mouth to laugh and laughter
fell from the television
I said to myself
it's almost better than real sugar
This happened yesterday as I traded
my own scalp for grain

Gold loaded our skulls
onto the backs of the born
and no credit was given
where no credit was due

Expectation
having grown so heavy
in its basement

*

In between accident and arrival
we are suspended
A significant horizon of downcast fire
in a public moment
my head tilted to the side
like, what?
The cogito
is the body
is nature
is the backward glancing continuum of Western history
writ in blood?

It's as if these winters have nothing on a chin
tilted upward
Speaking plainly, it is easier to tide
the lunar part
We are bound
and the world is what I can feel
up against this boundary
The sentence
becomes my future mail, my student debt,
these heads of nine crows I retreat
into storage

Scrolling through the temple of your name
I become locked into the commute of this
falling night
still dressed for the office

with my thighs awake
As if any art could reify
what time has taken away
The fact so brief I could not see
the temporal bind in front
of my face

*

History could be
my mother smoking in her truck
out a cracked window
The bluish greys eddying
toward escape
as all known stars accelerate
A bloodstream of dark matter
and the truth I'll never contain

In another history
a grandmother sleeps on a bed of hay
while the night sky screams a green light
of solar rays. Across the province
a grandmother picks burrs from her worn skirt
in a shack at the edge of the reserve.
A moose has been shot but where does she go
for her water?

Here I am filming my mother this past summer
demonstrating for a young cousin how to witch
for a well:

"Hold a saw by its edge with both hands
and bring the handle up to your chest
let it fall then count the bounces
that's how many feet down the water is"

*

The future history of mind
takes everything to forgive
the impulse to to rue the day
I met you at the university
I cannot make peace with that
which will not leave me
to test the surface tension
of deeper blues

If I hollow the morrow could you love me
as the poppet of your lost youth?

I can make an occasion of the hour known as 3 a.m.
for us to seep so readily into confusion

A young man pisses on the sidewalk in front of us
unknowingly
pushing a gasp up from his throat before he cuts
and runs down the residential street

Could it be that I've lived too long
with an idle mouth and my boots untied?

The bones of some medieval boy
discovered in the dying lips
of an uprooted tree
in the news today

Call me a taxi when the dawn is incendiary
The green of this could never have known me
not entirely

Dream apartments we could live in but never rent
The sun hunts me and everything I hold against my sense

SUPERPOSITION

Having surfaced could it be said
I came into self-consciousness
again through an act of purging?
Accessory to the second mind
housed in the middle, a neural web
around the viscera. Gut feelings
and heartbreak. I'm handed
some paper towels and a bottle
of Windex and told to clean up
after the half-wild dog that has
been living in our back porch. As
I open the door sunlight catches
in the bottle and projects a dancing
sapphire blue back into the hallway.
On the other side the dog has pissed
and defecated all over the floor.
He comes to greet me but the smell
is making me retch and I can't help
but throw up onto the mess. The dog
begins to lap up my sick, which makes
the whole thing worse and I retch again,
accidently vomiting on his flank which he
then bends his neck around to lick. It is in
this moment, at the age of seven, I believe
I had what psychoanalytic theorist
Julia Kristeva has called an experience
of abjection. A breakdown in the natural
order of things. A separation between the self
and an object of disgust that suggests death.

Somehow my mind was lifted up to the ceiling
and I could see myself with total vulnerability.
It wasn't just nausea that I felt in my stomach
but a true separation between myself
and the world; all its unpredictability
that I'd be tasked with weathering.

Seven is the canonical
age of reason, my grandmother
instructed me. Now that I am
cognitively responsible for
my sins I must confess them
in order to be in communion
with the divine and avoid hell
or purgatory; the waiting room
for souls. The confessional booth
was at the back of church, and I
had to walk past all the pews
of parishioners who watched me.
The booth smelled of adult
sweat and a man sat on the other
side of a little screen who would
forgive me.

I could never bring myself to say
that at a dinner party a father had
performed a magic trick where he
closed his hand around a small toy
and when he opened it again it was
gone. I asked if he could do the same
to me. He laughed nervously and said
he could try but he might not be able
to bring me back. I said that was okay
and from how his face fell I could tell
what I said was wrong. It was wrong
to want to be a part of nothingness.
Father, is it something dark in me
that wants to be held so close I
disappear permanently?

LETTER FROM HALIFAX

I just walked the street of my father. The street is called North.
I paused in front of his white apartment building as the sun
fed me from the west. There were two shopping carts chained
together, one from the liquor store. My father turned empty
bottles into full ones, into food and into rent. He pushed
his cart across the city gathering emptiness.

*

I wonder if the north was the repository of his best
intentions. He left when I was an infant.
Powerless over drink, he ran, jumped the track
and erased himself from public record.
He became a shadow I couldn't match.
Every Native man on the street, the unidentified
dead in government databases; I searched
their faces to see if they were a part of me.
Would-be astronomer in his youth, I'd learn
also to try and cast my gaze upwards.
When I look at the Pleiades I see seven sisters
who could hold me. In Anishinaabe cosmology
the constellation is known as Bagone'giizhig,
The-Hole-in-the-Sky.
A portal between this world and spirit.
Where I go when I dream
and, if anywhere, the place
I'll find him again.

*

I'm trying to write this
as I sit in a Tim Hortons
waiting to meet his
common-law spouse
who will give me some
of his personal effects
when a man next to me asks
what does this word mean?
pointing to a spot on the page
of a *Maclean's* where the word
'rapport' appears.

*

I landed yesterday in Halifax.
My aunt had called to say
he was here in hospital
with liver failure and in a coma.
The doctors would give him
forty-eight hours to come out of it.
I had the thought,
maybe
if I go to him
he'll wake up.

*

My father's skin had yellowed and the sclerae
of his eyes which were half open but clouded.
A tear slid from the corner of his right eye to past
the bone of his Indigenous cheek. This tear had not
yet dried when they began to withdraw life support,
machine by machine. What kept him breathing,
what jerked his head back and expanded his chest
with decreasing regularity was the last
to be withdrawn. A nurse said,
"He is in the process of actively dying now."

Actively dying.

*

In the ancient Near East a seer would look to
the stars or the livers of sheep for divination.
What does a liver show or hold? Spurinna
the haruspex foresaw the death of Caesar
in the entrails of a sacrifice. Paugak,
the cursed Anishinaabe skeleton
who flies through the boreal forest,
is said to consume the livers of his victims.
Prometheus' punishment for stealing fire
from the gods was to be chained to a rock
and have his liver torn out daily by an eagle.
Every night his liver would regenerate.

*

Two days have now passed. Two days I have been
in Halifax. Two days since my father has passed
from mystery into appearance, laying bare
his totality on a death bed, distended cirrhotic belly
and ethereally beautiful face. He passed from unknowing
into eternity as I watched the neon lines above him lie flat.
I am still watching. I still do not know what I know. A nor'easter
now passing over me, spilling its moisture from the Atlantic,
heavy rain that by midnight may turn to snow.

*

What does it mean to actively die? Actively?
I've been reading Knausgaard who writes:
For the heart, life is simple: it beats for as long
as it can. Then it stops. Full stop as in a period,
as a period is a flat line when extended. I have been
given my father's papers, his Polaroids and a pocket watch
that belonged to my great-grandfather. I have been
given his ball cap that kept the Maritime sun
out of his eyes as he scavenged for bottles.
The band of this hat has collected his scent
which is lemongrass, earth, and discount smoke.
I have been given his small tools, cologne, nail
clippers, a water canister, a small plastic box of razors,

a picture of me as a baby, a drawing of electrical currents,
a knife.

*

I'm here, wedged within three nor'easters.
The first fell after he died. The jaundice,
the eyes that are mine, the snow a whiteout
of every street. The third will come Tuesday
and cover Halifax in a foot of lace. Today I
bought *Ocean* by Sue Goyette, a black dress
and a pair of tights. Today I ate berries
and drank black coffee. Today I felt
the harbour folding in. A sphere flinched
in my portal vein. Today I woke up late.
This evening I looked up at the constellation
Orion, Biboonikeonini, The Winter-Maker.
Tomorrow I will see my father's body for the last time.
Tuesday he will become ash.
Become ash.
Actively.

FATHER'S DAY

The undertaker doesn't warn you

about the consistency of the ashes.

Not like those of say, a cigarette.

Scattering them will not be like

when you used to blow into

the ashtrays at your grandparents'

house as if blowing the fluff off

of dandelions gone to seed, for

which you were gently scolded.

The human form is difficult to destroy

utterly. When fragments of your father's

bones thud against the ground of his wishing

forgive yourself for the shock, the momentary

turn in your stomach. When you see that his ash

has caught onto your shoes and leggings and skin

come to see this as your first and only embrace.

SPRING LETTER

Waabooz,
tracking through the last of snow
love is a root I stumble over
in search of you.

Geese fly backwards in my mind,
a rewind that a stand of tamaracks
sees just perfectly:

there is no way to trap
the anxious rabbit of me
as my hide also reorders itself
inside the brush of wide time.

PHYSICAL ANTHROPOLOGY

The day was leaf litter

and excess packaging.

If I was the choked woman

in the centre of Kahlo's bathtub,

it is also the obscene contract

of the Americas that renders me

startling from my poverty. Yet I eclipsed

a vacant limb no less hymnal no less vernal

in being partial.

Unequivocal redux of

what would hold me to the doorframe

of this convenience store where I try

to buy a calling card

to reach a future of white lilies.

Lilies called help and lilies called friend.

Lilies called to testify against myself.

Economy of the unheard-of

an impure dish of womanhood.

Fully gynecological.

Gradually increase the dose.

I resurfaced before I was ready

to inherit the flare of True North.

Startling for my limits.

A new hominin imprint.

I know you know

women too painted those novels

in the caves of Lascaux.

LIFE CYCLE OF THE ANIMAL CALLED SHE

	I ascended not through grace but via debt. A trick
Wife	of red knew its way all through me. How to cure him
Mother	of the colic, the bed wet, the conquest, or the lack
Mistress	of consent? I haven't got it in my purse, in my nerve,
	or in a hospice of milk. A lactic dew stripping the patina

	from my femurs. Had I another beginning I'd have
Waitress	taken love down from its shelf and inserted it. The century
Nurse	that flattered me begged also in roses and spring. I am
Whore	but a sinner ever retreating. The limits of my language
	are the limits of my world. And the word was final beyond
	a reasonable doubt.

Breaking down before the reliquary age I have this sense
I am between genders in the west end of this dying city.
Maid To be a ram bucking in the stars. Did I miscarry the accident?
Maiden Out on my own release and flaunting recognizance. I palpated
Crone the grief. Made a mask of all the features that are receding.
The bones my dual nature disclosed amid a lawn of cosmos.

There is an amber-coloured skull in the painting called *Vanitas*
that is my son. My son cannot speak because I have no son.
Birth I have a brother on the spectrum. He drives a rig hauling metals.
Marriage He is my brother but we do not share a father. It is impolite
Grave to speak of such things. My headstone could read that I was
a creature unafraid to breathe these titles into speech.

Subpoena my belief. Love doesn't work here anymore.
I lifted my face into distraction. I lifted my hair at its roots,
my breasts with wires. When I dreamt the Indian Agent
he was the accountant of persuasion. I let down my limbs

Address   and replicated. I do not know any other door through
Occupation which to enter. Castigate my own body in service to
Age   the tyranny of will which is no altar. There is no take
away in the forest. Who will be invited to eat and devise
a plot of land? Make this mantle disappear: the world
is independent of my will. I've said this. Nothing in me
can ever truly pay the lease.

SUPERPOSITION

The
red
I
perceive
is
daylight
filtering
through
the
capillaries
of
my
eyelids
before
they
open
into
a
void
on
the
edge
of
the
city

from
a
bare
mattress
I
hear
a
man's
voice
like
a
passing
freight
saying
that
he
will
end
me
if
I
don't
behave

a
mark
darkening
on
the
inside
of
my
arm
the
size
of
a
thumb
where
another
universe
collided
with
this
one

if
I
don't
survive
this
I
worry
what
will
he
do
with
me
what
if
no
one
can
ever
even
find
my
body?

TRUE VALUE

The sky was never my court date.

If I died once. If I left the body.

Habeas corpus.

This is not my grave.

The value in a dead woman

is that she cannot be killed

again or cross-examined.

The value in being the dead

woman at trial is the Crown

doesn't represent you

regardless.

The value in being

dead is that it's impolite

to speak ill

of you.

What is called

wellness,

victim-witness?

A swab taken

of every orifice.

Were there any

identifying marks?

Were you in fact

on the moon

that night,

Miss Howard?

Did you make a choice?

I made a cut—it released something.

I broke the line.

BRAIN MAPPING

I might sit in a chair and watch as a stranger's brain appears
on the screen, slice by slice. I could plot a correlate of thoughts.
Still I will never know you, only myself in relation. A rape in every
generation of my line within the time of photography. A heritable
loom of methylated DNA. How to speak this quiet violence that has
separated me from history? Have I made myself accessible
enough?

There is a real power in the semipermeable.
Danger of the underbelly exposed. Tripwires
of any tree rooting itself to the ground. In the forest
I would often trip where the roots surfaced in partial
relief against the pine needles. Smelling of sifted
blood in full summer, iron oxides, ochre.
Now I paint my body with Sephora.

*

Exhaustion is a hall
of waiting
I think because
I am a feeling thing
a thing
inside entropy

Neural effigy
what is it to be found
innocent
or at least not guilty?

With my health in my hand
at the end of this
inverted hospital
I make a sign of the cross
over the lack
of applause

*

I set out in my work dress into the back seat of a stranger's car. "A beautiful day," in an accent I can't place. The worn spillage of North York goes on in burnt umber brickwork. And I have myself become a stranger.

When I enter the hospital I see Kafka's face. He stares out at me from a silk-screen in Warhol's "Ten Portraits of Jews of the Twentieth Century" series gifted by a community member. Sometimes the lobby is filled with the smell of frankincense and the sound of women singing in Hebrew. Many of the eldest elderly came here as children after the war, survivors. This is a place of final refuge and a place where I assist with research into the cognitive mechanisms of the living human brain.

The walls of the upper floors of the research wing feature work by Inuit and Native American artists. On Fridays, after the lab meeting, I will stare into the eyes of a man's portrait, an unnamed warrior who resembles my great-grandfather. My great-grandfather fought in the First World War. I was able to get a pdf of his war records off of a genealogy site. He was shot in the back in France. The bullet just a few inches shy of his heart. I later learn his sons also fought in the Second World War and what they saw left them unable to speak any of it. One uncle took what he couldn't say to the train that killed him. I scattered my father above those tracks.

History is a sewing motion
along a thin membrane.

Pia mater.
Dura mater.
Tender mother.
Hard mother.

Can I still learn
to feel protected
by what encloses me?

*

I've cast my lot
deadheaded into
an estuary Monday
a split hare
efficacious
at the dam's ready
my timber silt hard
cast tributaries
a brother's ideation
among the earth
metals slighted
rivulets
of nickel ore
smelted sulphuric
for years before
he was born
I've got promises
and roses
and plastic
amber cylinders
for remedy

I've got to ask a question with lichen in it
my hair with streaks of caribou moss in it
give it up
my bad ankles
and wet temperament

*

I dreamt this morning
of a worm, near translucent
evacuated from a wound in
my side not unlike the last
wound of Christ and I thought
this is the howling worm
who with his dark secret love
would my life have destroyed
because yesterday I obsessed
over Blake's "The Sick Rose"
recited it five times, the Five
Holy Wounds, the invisible worm
that flies through the howling
storm of Blake, and I thought
that worm itself is howling
a howling worm that rests
in a bed of crimson joy
as a wound is a rose
flesh bloomed as belief
and I dreamt also of a poet
who was a prophet and I went
with her and others to Coney Island
a place I've never been
and we climbed into the bucket
seats of a ride to hear her speak
about the motion of the stars,
charmed quarks, how to
distill reality into intention

and some women learned
this secret and began to flip
atomically, simultaneously
changing positions with each other
a man appeared on the fairground
with a rifle and fired high calibre rounds
at their faces but almost instantaneous
to the moment of impact the damage
would be rearranged as if nothing
had happened, a reversal of physical
change, over and over again
my younger brother appeared
as a small boy and caught a bullet
to the forehead and I only knew
enough to heal this one wound
in order to return him
to the world

*

As a child sometimes
I would receive a flick
to the centre of my
forehead. A flick
to the skin above
the skull bone
that houses
the frontal pole
a site in concert
with other structures
that is said to synthesize
the present tense
I experience as me.

*

Brief habits,
minor passions,
ill-considered missives
into the drain of days.
Always it is like this:

thrumming to my own dark frequency
like a broken lark under
a maple tree.

. . .

*

All the night assembles my subject.
All the night, the shape of one's self.

And what do you find there
beyond the quiet and the dark?
That I was to do away with all of it
yet decided to remain.

Reforge myself inside tomorrow's humidex.
Aslant and listless, answer the messages,
order eggs and begin again.

I must pursue the future
pulling dawn through
through the needle
point of compass north.

Make me the sort
of animal who knows
when to take cover.

A shaking dress.
My hide blazing
in the territory
of the truly sensate.

THIS NOCTURNE WENT SUMMER

Expectant ions
in the wettest summer
on record
having neither god
nor country
nor countenance
I should project my drowning
into the heronry.

        Little clusters
           of rust

               coagulate
               my veins

               such is the feeling.

Epigenetic pearls of unending drive
sometimes I find myself horrid like Proust,
like Kafka or Nanabozho, given to moods
and vapors and sickness. What cannot stand
because I am female and therefore suspect,
furtive, unruly. I think sometimes there is
something of Arendt or Curie or the Moon
in me and also every woman I meet living
on the streets. The uncertainty of me driving
a hot spark into the centre of my solar plexus
such that I cannot tell the difference between
failure and illness.

> Capital milks
> its stress cortisol
> to grow a horror in the body.

> It finds us all.

Time knows what it does or it doesn't,
is it truly a sequence that is continuing?
I might suck time from the ridge of your lips.
I think, the city negates me? Yes and no.
The mess I've made of things. I'm given
to the question mark, the ellipsis.
The future has already happened
and I understand nothing. A child
cries on the street and the mother
answers, "I don't care." Another
woman walking past in expensive
spandex says into her phone,
"whatever I have risked I stand
to earn." I cannot hunt. I lock
       the door when you go away
         with my love and then with fern
         in hand I stand recalcitrant. I am bogged.
       A pustule of astrocytes. It is possible
         the rest has ended.

I brought the vena cava as far as
postponing the present.

Here is the list:
the date,
the face,
the hour.

Soft courage,
I miss my ever-so-refined
smooth exit
concomitant
contour kit.

Breath became
a danger set in endocrine relief.
A sweet antiquity outside of sin.

Modest head
who has yet to pilfer your coffers?
Stonewall green as any word when
I come to and the popcorn ceiling
is a testimony I can't understand.

At work a superconducting magnet
lulls in its hull below the hospital.
A hungry field of probability where
each observer is a privileged centre.
I keep getting lost in the halls
while the last suture of my skull
closes its account.

I dream of places I have lived before
in which I am an unremarkable agent.
Every screen is a stun gun, a spent stud.
I scroll as from the non-place of a lobotomy.
At night I place a pressed note of melatonin
under my soul and pray for a repeat.

The day was disinterested in me.

I can't simply be the secretary of this
contagion that loosed me upon the world
with so many holes that must be probed
and assessed for progress. I can't offer my
recent kill as a solvent or an antidote. I could
take your mouth as I can't help but take
your mouth out of the stillborn word
and render it a new communion. Am I
a disaster about my nerves? Outside of
you, waiting for my humors to run clear,
a colonial notion. So said my affection
a lining of greenery within
the posture.

Late Summer.
I swing it like the spirit that comes
out of my mouth, the aggregate
of my mouth a sit-in. I am congregating
in an alcove, an achronological history
of tones, as if I already knew the answer.
Purchased the derivative, the transform,
all sinusoidal descriptions of mercenary light.
The desperation that exits me is not truth
but surface. Can I spend the night? Can I
spend the whole surface
in one night?

Memory stalks
all axons and familiar haunts.
Incisors against your lower lip,
a brainstem connection
that potentiates all want and loss.
Everything we like to think is possible
in art. Without a kind of gruesome beauty,
I'd said, then—why not? My boxes packed
full of smudged ink and simply living
exhausts me. The remainders I stack,
cold compress resemblances. The lack
in my language [redacts] me. The sprung
brain of a creature under duress.
A name I call myself. What is it
that John Clare wrote?
I am the self-consumer of my woes?
Runnin' through the 6 with my woes?

Ontario,
will you remember my face, my debts,
my attempts at excellence?
As for the rest who passed
through me like silt did you forget
when I said
that the best
is yet?

Do I intend an extended meditation
on the impossibility of object relations
so late in the game? The lesser pox
that rests in me a deep, cold water
lake.

All the skins

a fibrous silk

of nerve stimulus

wedded to infinity

the sky has a nickel sheen

false rapids and birch and bottle caps in an old code of surety

each day I wake and rewrite
this and in doing so
destroy my memory

I mined an intracranial system
of service roads. I mined the woods.

When your hand crested the iliac of my hip
and took up this branch, a whip
of lilac. The jurisdiction of my heart
a fall of red clovers
all over the township.

Let this dark summer
displace the original hour
of our mutual birth.
What reappears here

the night I crossed out

The 'cosmic bruise,' also known as the cosmic microwave background (CMB) cold spot, is an anomalous region detected in the "heat map" of the known universe. Recent interpretations of the data related to the CMB cold spot give weight to the theory that it was caused by the collision of a parallel universe early in our universe's formation (see "Evidence against a supervoid causing the CMB Cold Spot" (MacKenzie et al., 2017)).

"Noli turbare circulos meos," a phrase often translated as *do not disturb my circles*, is said to have been the last words of Greek mathematician Archimedes, referencing some geometric work he was doing in sand, before he was murdered by Roman soldiers.

I first encountered the Anishinaabe cosmological knowledge present in this book at a REDTalk called "Stars and Sky Stories: Indigenous Cosmology and Western Astronomy" that took place in Toronto on May 31, 2018. Further research was informed by the work of educator Michael Wassegijig Price and the book *Ojibwe Sky Star Map—Constellation Guide* by Annette S. Lee, William Wilson, Jeffrey Tibbetts, and Carl Gawboy.

"For the heart, life is simple: it beats for as long as it can. Then it stops" is from Karl Ove Knausgaard's *A Death in the Family: My Struggle Book I* (Trans. Don Bartlett).

"The limits of my language are the limits of my world" and "the world is independent of my will" are from *Tractatus Logico-Philosophicus* by Ludwig Wittgenstein.

"This is not my grave" is from Anne Boyer's poem WHAT RESEMBLES THE GRAVE BUT ISN'T.

"A heritable loom of methylated DNA," refers to an epigenetic biochemical process whereby the environmental experience of an organism can result in changes to how genes are expressed in future offspring. It has been hypothesized as one possible mechanism of intergenerational trauma.

Nanabozho is an Anishinaabe culture hero and trickster figure who often appears in both human and rabbit form.

Astrocytes are star-shaped cells present in the brain and spinal cord.

"Each day I wake and rewrite/this and in doing so/destroy my memory" is directly inspired by remarks given by Jacques Roubaud during an interview with *BOMB* Magazine regarding the writing process for his novels *The Great Fire of London: A Story with Interpolations and Bifurcations* and *The Loop*.

"I am the self-consumer of my woes" is from John Clare's poem "I Am!".

"Runnin' through the 6 with my woes," is a lyric from Drake's "Know Yourself."

For words in Anishinaabemowin: a sufficiently attentive reading will reveal any word's English equivalent.

ACKNOWLEDGEMENTS

I am very grateful to have received funding for the completion of this book from the Canada Council for the Arts, the Ontario Arts Council, the Toronto Arts Council, and Access Copyright.

I was incredibly fortunate to write and grow with students during residencies at the University of British Columbia Kelowna Indigenous Arts Intensive, the University of Calgary, the Leighton Arts Studios at the Banff Centre for Creativity, Douglas College, Sheridan College, and *The Capilano Review*.

Previous iterations of poems in this collection have appeared in the following publications: *Action, Spectacle, Best Canadian Poetry 2018, Camera Austria, Canadian Art, The Capilano Review, CV2, Determinants of Indigenous Peoples Health Second Edition, DUSIE, The Fiddlehead, The Humber Literary Review, New Poetry, The Next Wave An Anthology of 21st Century Writing, Poetry Magazine, The Puritan, The Walrus,* and *The West End Phoenix*. Kind thanks to the editors for including my work.

This book's coming into the world is due to the brilliant and generous guidance of my editor Dionne Brand. Thank you for believing in my writing when I felt could not. Thank you for the time needed to rear this errant child. Thank you for demonstrating how "poetry can make a life" in all you do.

Thank you to Kelly Joseph and all others at M&S who carried me along with impossible patience and kindness. Thanks also to my agent Stephanie Sinclair who helped shepherd the book towards realization.

Gratitude to my friends John Bell, Jimmy McInnes, and Kaitlin Purcell for supportive feedback on early drafts.

My ancestors. My family. My friends. My peers. My students. Neither I nor this work would exist without you. I wasn't sure I could survive the writing of this and having to write it through some of the most tumultuous and dark years of my life, but you kept me afloat. Everything good I have to give is the result of the incredible community of people I have around me. I could never name each one of you here. Please know that my gratitude is boundless.

Great thanks, chi-miigwetch, to you the reader for spending this probability with me.

Ralph Kolewe

LIZ HOWARD's debut collection *Infinite Citizen of the Shaking Tent* won the 2016 Griffin Poetry Prize, was shortlisted for the 2015 Governor General's Award for poetry, and was named a *Globe and Mail* top 100 book. Her poetry has appeared in *Canadian Art*, *The Fiddlehead*, *Poetry Magazine*, and *Best Canadian Poetry 2018*. Howard received an Honours Bachelor of Science with High Distinction from the University of Toronto, and an MFA in Creative Writing from the University of Guelph. She is of mixed settler and Anishinaabe heritage. Born and raised on Treaty 9 territory in northern Ontario, she currently lives in Toronto.